First World War
and Army of Occupation
War Diary
France, Belgium and Germany

49 DIVISION
147 Infantry Brigade,
Brigade Trench Mortar Battery
1 April 1916 - 31 August 1916

WO95/2802/3

The Naval & Military Press Ltd
www.nmarchive.com
Published in association with The National Archives

Published by

The Naval & Military Press Ltd

Unit 10 Ridgewood Industrial Park,

Uckfield, East Sussex,

TN22 5QE England

Tel: +44 (0) 1825 749494

www.naval-military-press.com

www.nmarchive.com

This diary has been reprinted in facsimile from the original. Any imperfections are inevitably reproduced and the quality may fall short of modern type and cartographic standards.

© Crown Copyright
Images reproduced by permission of The National Archives, London, England, 2015.

Contents

Document type	Place/Title	Date From	Date To
Heading	WO95/2802 147 Bde 49 Div Bde Trench Mortar Apr 16-Aug 16		
Heading	49th Division 147th Infy Bde Trench Mortar Bty 1916 Apl Aug 1916		
Miscellaneous	147th T.M.B. June July And August 1916		
War Diary	Toutencourt (Lens 11)	01/04/1916	08/04/1916
War Diary	Naours (Lens 11)	08/04/1916	15/04/1916
War Diary	Toutencourt (Lens 11)	15/04/1916	29/04/1916
War Diary	Naours (Lens 11)	29/04/1916	16/05/1916
War Diary	Querrier Amiens 17	17/05/1916	17/05/1916
War Diary	Naours Lens 11	18/05/1916	26/05/1916
War Diary	Wargneiss Lens 11	27/05/1916	30/05/1916
War Diary	Naours Lens 11	31/05/1916	31/05/1916
War Diary	Rubempre Lens 11	31/05/1916	31/05/1916
War Diary	Martinsart	12/06/1916	13/06/1916
War Diary	Aveluy	14/06/1916	30/06/1916
War Diary	Aveluy & Trenches	01/07/1916	01/07/1916
War Diary	S. Bluff-Aveluy Johnstone's Post	02/07/1916	02/07/1916
War Diary	Johnstone's Post Paisley Av. Aveluy Wood	03/07/1916	03/07/1916
War Diary	Aveluy Wood Thiepval Sector Aveluy	04/07/1916	06/07/1916
War Diary	Aveluy Wood	08/07/1916	15/07/1916
War Diary	Leipsig Salient	15/07/1916	25/07/1916
War Diary	Peterhead Sap	26/07/1916	31/07/1916
Heading	147th Brigade 49th Division 147th Light Trench Mortar Battery August 1916		
War Diary	Thiepval (Left Sector)	01/08/1916	28/08/1916
War Diary	Thiepval Left Sector Arqueves	20/08/1916	21/08/1916
War Diary	Thiepval Left Sector Arqueves Forceville	27/08/1916	27/08/1916
War Diary	Forceville	28/08/1916	29/08/1916
War Diary	Thiepval (Right)	30/08/1916	31/08/1916

WO95/2802

147 BDE   49 DIV.

BDE TRENCH MORTAR
Apr '16 – Aug '16

(3)

49TH DIVISION
147TH INFY BDE

TRENCH MORTAR BTY

1916 APL ~~JUN~~ - AUG 1916L

147th T.M.B.

June, July and August 1916.

1st Cavalry Bgde
2nd Car Bgde G
4th Dragoon Gds
9th Lancers
18th Hussars

August to
Decb 1914
Decb 1914

"1" R.H.A. 20th to 19/13/14.
"L" R.H.A. 20th to 19/13/14.

WAR DIARY
or
INTELLIGENCE SUMMARY.

(Erase heading not required.)

Army Form C. 2118.

Place	Date	Hour	Summary of Events and Information	Remarks and references to Appendices
			Nil	

30/4/16

Wallis, Lt
o/c 147 T.M.B.
49th Div

147/2
TRENCH MORTAR BATTERY.

Army Form C. 2118

WAR DIARY T.M XLIX
or
INTELLIGENCE SUMMARY   147/2 Trench Mortar Battery

Vol 1

Place	Date	Hour	Summary of Events and Information	Remarks and references to Appendices
TOUTENCOURT (LENS II.)	1-4-16	3-30 p.m.	147/2 T. M. Battery formed at School of Mortars X Corps. Personnel of battery, 2 officers, 5 N.C.Os, 18 men. JCA.	elle
"	1-4-16 to 8-4-16		Training of battery at School of Mortars X Corps. JCA.	
"	8-4-16	1 p.m.	Departure for Naours. JCA.	
Naours (LENS II)	8-4-16	3 p.m.	Arrive at Naours. JCA.	
"	9-4-16	6 p.m.	Transfer 2 N.C.Os + 7 men to 147/1 T. M. Battery + receive 2 N.C.Os + 7 men in exchange. JCA.	
"	10-4-16		Four hours Gun Drill, two hours Route March. JCA.	
"	11-4-16		One hour rifle drill, three hour gun drill, two hour route march. Two men moved to hospital. JCA.	
"	12-4-16		Half an hour squad drill, one hour kit inspection, two hours gun drill, two hours route march. JCA.	
"	13-4-16		Half an hour saluting drill, one hour physical drill, two hour gun drill, two hours road reconnaissance. JCA.	
"	14-4-16		Half an hour gas helmet drill, one hour squad drill, two hour gun drill, one hour physical drill. JCA.	

Kenneth Ackroyd Lt.
O.C. 147/2 T. M. Battery.

Army Form C. 2118

147/2 Trench Mortar Battery

WAR DIARY
or
INTELLIGENCE SUMMARY
(Erase heading not required.)

Instructions regarding War Diaries and Intelligence Summaries are contained in F. S. Regs., Part II. and the Staff Manual respectively. Title Pages will be prepared in manuscript.

Place	Date	Hour	Summary of Events and Information	Remarks and references to Appendices
Naours (Lens 11)	12-4-16	12.30 p.m.	Departure for School of Mortars X Corps. at Toutencourt. K.A.	
Toutencourt (Lens 11)	"	3-15 p.m.	Arrive at School of Mortars X Corps, TOUTENCOURT. K.A.	
"	16-4-16 to 29-4-16		At School of Mortars X Corps. assisting in instruction of reinforcements. K.A.	
"	17-4-16		One man proceeds to Hospital. K.A.	
"	25-4-16		One man returns from Hospital. K.A.	
"	29-4-16	1 p.m.	Departure for NAOURS. K.A.	
Naours (Lens 11)	"	3 p.m.	Arrive at NAOURS. One man returns from Hospital. K.A.	
"	30-4-16	9 a.m.	Church Parade. K.A.	

Kenneth Ackroyd Lt.
O.C. 147/2 Trench Mortar Battery.

WAR DIARY or INTELLIGENCE SUMMARY

Army Form C. 2118

XLIX

147/2 TRENCH MORTAR BATTERY.

Vol 2

Place	Date	Hour	Summary of Events and Information	Remarks and references to Appendices
NAOURS LENS II	May 1st		One hour's Squad Drill, 3 hrs Gun Drill, 1 hr route march.	JH
"	" 2nd		One hour's squad drill, 3 hrs Gun Drill, 1 hr route march	JH
"	" 3rd		Rifle Drill one hr, 3 hrs Gun Drill, 1 hr route march.	JH
"	" 4th		One hr. Physical Drill & 1 hr. emplacement digging, 1 hr. Gun Drill	JH
"	" 5th		One hr. Physical Drill. Bde. manoeuvres (cancelled owing to rain)	JH
"	" 6th		One hr. Physical Drill, 1 hr. Gun drill 2 hrs. Emplacement digging	JH
"	" 7th		Physical Drill, 1 hr. Tactical scheme, 1 hr. Gun drill	JH
"	" 8th		Physical Drill 1 hr. Tactical scheme, 1 hr. Gun drill	JH
"	" 9th		Physical Drill 1 hr. Emplacement digging, 1 hr Gun drill	JH
"	" 10th		Physical Drill 1 hr. Tactical scheme, 1 hr route march	JH
"	" 11th		Physical Drill 1 hr. 1 hr. Emplacement digging, 2 hrs Gun drill	JH
"	" 12th		Physical Drill 1 hr, 4 hrs Tactical Scheme.	JH
"	" 13th		Physical Drill & Tactical Scheme & firing. 2hrs Emplacement Digging	JH
"	" 14th		One officer Lt. R. Arbogast admitted to hospital	JH
"	" 15th		2/Lt. D. E. Tyall attached to Battery.	JH
"	" 15th		Physical Drill. Firing Practice & Tactical scheme 4hrs, 2 hrs	JH
"	" 16		One hr. Physical Drill. emplacement digging	JH
			Demonstration Rehearsal for demonstration at Fourth Army } JH
QUERRIEU AMIENS 17	" 17th		at Fourth Army Headquarters.	JH
NAOURS LENS II	" 18		Physical Drill, Tactical scheme shooting practice 1 hr, 2 hrs Emplacement Digging	JH

Army Form C. 2118

1472
TRENCH MORTAR
BATTERY
No.

WAR DIARY
or
INTELLIGENCE SUMMARY
(Erase heading not required.)

Instructions regarding War Diaries and Intelligence Summaries are contained in F. S. Regs., Part II. and the Staff Manual respectively. Title Pages will be prepared in manuscript.

Place	Date	Hour	Summary of Events and Information	Remarks and references to Appendices.
NAOURS LENS II	May 19th		Physical Drill & hr. Tactical scheme, rapid firing & judging J.A. distance, 2 hrs route march.	
"	" 20th		1hr Route March, 3 hrs Emplacement Digging J.A.	
"	" 21st		Physical Drill & 1hr Gun drill & Emplacement digging, 1hr man. J.A.	
"	" 23rd		1hr Physical drill, & hr practice firing & Emplacement digging, 1hr J.A. Glavaphone	
"	" 24th		Physical Drill & hr Tactical scheme & firing, 2 hrs Bayonet J.A. Fighting	
"	" 25th		Physical Drill, & hr Tactical scheme & firing J.A.	
"	" 26th		Physical Drill Tactical scheme & firing & hr, 1hr Bayonet J.A. Fighting	
WARGNIES LENS II	" 27th		Digging emplacements shell-holes for Gun Emplacements. J.A.	
"	" 28th		Digging for demonstration. J.A.	
"	" 30th	10.30am	Swearing in of dummy wheel holes & regiving J.A.	
NAOURS LENS II	" 31st	2.30pm	Demonstration of Stokes mortars followed by infantry J.A. attack.	
RUBEMPRÉ LENS II	" 31st	5.30pm	Marched from Naours to Rubempré J.A. Arrived at Rubempré & Billeted J.A.	

J. Hargreaves 2nd Lieut
O/C 147/2 Trench Mortar Battery
2 May 31st 16

1875 Wt. W593/826 1,000,000 4/15 J.B.C. & A. A.D.S.S./Forms/C. 2118.

Army Form C. 2118.

2118-9

147 T M Bde

Vol 3744

WAR DIARY
or
INTELLIGENCE SUMMARY.

(Erase heading not required.)

Instructions regarding War Diaries and Intelligence Summaries are contained in F.S. Regs., Part II. and the Staff Manual respectively. Title pages will be prepared in manuscript.

Place	Date	Hour	Summary of Events and Information	Remarks and references to Appendices
	1916			
MARTINSART	June 12		Amalgamation of 147/1 & 147/2 T.M. Batteries	RW
do	13		Training	RW
AVELUY	14	4.30 pm	Left MARTINSART for AVELUY attached 32nd Divn from date.	RW
do	14/30 inclusive		Attached 32nd Division as working & carrying parties	RW

H.H.Hammond
for O.C. 147th T.M.B.

T134. Wt. W708—776. 500000. 4/15. Sir J. C. & S.

WAR DIARY
or
INTELLIGENCE SUMMARY.
(Erase heading not required.)

Army Form C. 2118.

Instructions regarding War Diaries and Intelligence Summaries are contained in F. S. Regs., Part II. and the Staff Manual respectively. Title pages will be prepared in manuscript.

Place	Date	Hour	Summary of Events and Information	Remarks and references to Appendices
AVELUY & Trenches	1916 July 1	7.25 am	Right Section assisted 32nd Division in preliminary bombardment. Left Section at AVELUY in reserve. 400 rounds fired. Right Section withdrawn 5.30 pm & placed under command G.O.C. 147 Bde.	Div. Div.
			Right Section took up position on S. BLUFF. Left Section remained at AVELUY. No casualties.	Div. Div.
S. BLUFF - AVELUY	2		Right Section S. BLUFF. Left Section & reinforcements left AVELUY 10.30 am. & took up their position at S. BLUFF also. The whole Battery moved, together with their reinforcements, into position at JOHNSTONE'S POST 11 pm & remained there until 7.30 am the morning of 3rd.	Div. Div.
JOHNSTONE'S POST			2243 Pte HARDY, W. admitted to Hospital sick.	Div. Div.
JOHNSTONE'S POST	3		Left JOHNSTONE'S POST 7.30 am & under orders in dug-outs in PAISLEY AVENUE until 1 pm. when Battery proceeded to AVELUY WOOD – ASSEMBLY TRENCHES (C. GROUP) where they remained for the night.	Div. Div.
PAISLEY AV. AVELUY WOOD				Div.
AVELUY WOOD, THIEPVAL SECTOR, AVELUY.	4	4.30 pm	Left Section proceeded to trenches THIEPVAL SECTOR. Right Section proceeded to AVELUY.	Div.
	5		Remained in THIEPVAL SECTOR & Right Section at AVELUY.	Div.
	6	6 pm	Right Section relieved Left Section the relieved section returning to AVELUY.	Div.
	7	8 pm	Right Section relieved & proceeded to AVELUY WOOD. L. Section & reinforcements joining them at 12 midnight 7/8 July, in ASSEMBLY TRENCHES GROUP "B" for the night.	Div.

WAR DIARY
INTELLIGENCE SUMMARY.
(Erase heading not required.)

Army Form C. 2118.

Place	Date	Hour	Summary of Events and Information	Remarks and references to Appendices
	1916			
AVELUY WOOD	July 8	8 a.m.	Moved from GROUP "B" to GROUP "C" ASSEMBLY TRENCHES	—
		2 p.m.	ASSEMBLY TRENCHES to SOUTH BLUFF attached 146 Brigade.	—
		3.30 p.m.	Relieved 146 T.M.B. on right & left flank of LEIPSIC REDOUBT; 6 guns in all 3 on the right & 3 on the left.	—
	8/15		Took over the above position for this period	—
			CASUALTIES 10 July 2160 L/Cpl Spring T. Art. Right Returned to duty	—
			" 12 " 1346 Cpl Woods, W. Art. "	—
			" 12 " 2509 Pte Bowers, A. Art. Evacuated to ENGLAND	—
			" 12 " 2222 Cpl Wilkinson E. Art. — " —	—
			" 12 " 2160 L/Cpl Spring T. Shell Shock Returned to duty	—
			" 12 " 3394 Pte W. — do —	—
			" 12 " 4227 North, A. — do —	—
			" 12 " 3336 O'Hara, A. — do —	—
			" 12 " 2/Lt Lyall Q.C. slightly wounded — do — Evacuated to ENGLAND.	—
LEIPSIC SALIENT 15/23			Relieved 146 T.M.B. for the purpose of assisting in defence of LEIPSIC SALIENT.	—
			Fired 800 rounds four right.	—
	16 July		CASUALTIES 3066 Pte Dickinson, C. Art. EVACUATED to BASE	—
			4504 Pte Davis, E. Art. KILLED	—

WAR DIARY
or
INTELLIGENCE SUMMARY.
(Erase heading not required.)

Army Form C. 2118.

Place	Date	Hour	Summary of Events and Information	Remarks and references to Appendices
	July 23/5		Attached to 148 Infty Bgde	Ref
			CASUALTIES 3 Ptes Becker	Ref
	25		Relieved 148 T.M.B. in THIEPVAL LEFT SECTOR & came under the orders of the G.O.C. (147 Infty Bgde). During the afternoon till 6 p.m. there was a very	Ref
			heavy enemy artillery bombardment from HAMEL to ALBERT	Ref
PETERHEAD SAP	26	6 p.m.	Enemy minenwerfer activity on our left; we fired 54 rounds in retaliation, silencing his fire.	Ref
	27		Ordinary trench warfare, fetching ammunition, building recesses, strengthening fire positions & hipping emplacements	Ref
	28		do - & cleaning guns, ammunition etc	Ref
	29		do -	Ref
PETERHEAD SAP	30	7.30 p.m.	Fired 30 rounds to cover fire heavy F.M. in response to further MINENWERFER activity against Dinton on our left	Ref
	31		Same work as on 27th	Ref

A.J.Wilmerood
for O.C. 147 T.M.B.

147th Brigade.
49th Division

147th LIGHT TRENCH MORTAR BATTERY

AUGUST 1 9 1 6

WAR DIARY
or
INTELLIGENCE SUMMARY
(Erase heading not required.)

Army Form C. 2118.

Place	Date	Hour	Summary of Events and Information	Remarks and references to Appendices
THIEPVAL (LEFT SECTOR)	Aug 1	6.40 a.m. 6.7 a.m.	In conjunction with Artillery we fired from our positions in PETERHEAD, PETERHEAD SAP, GOOROCK STREET and HAMILTON AVENUE.	
	2/4		Ordinary trench warfare and shafting positions, cleaning ammunition & guns &c., & in reply to enemy retaliation after a smoke display on the evening of the 4th we fired 100 rounds.	
	5		Fired 50 rounds	
	6	6.30 a.m.	In the PETERHEAD Junction enemy minenwerfers were firing in the direction of 17 C & D (Ref. Map 57 D S.E. 1/20000) In conjunction with the heavy T.M's & our T.B. plus we retaliated firing 270 rounds doing considerable damage to enemy machine gun emplacements, parapet & trench vs. HAMILTON AV. & GOOROCK ST. position firing 50 rounds in each O.P & M.G. emplacements 5	
		8.15 p.m	Enemy open fired minenwerfers at 17 D 7.4 but left our patrol out & did not fire	
	7/19		Between these dates we had orders not to fire on ordinary occasions owing to there being very large working parties out. On the extreme left junction we collected 5 Gas ammunition from Sap & various places where it had been dumped on 1 July; had recesses built in tunnels 5 & 6, supplied working parties to remove in sandbags debris & bones from tunnels, had working parties at THIEPVAL MAGAZINE & ROOT CASTLE detaching rounds until we had 2,500 rounds stacked cleaned & ready in both magazines & 2000 in each tunnel stacked in recesses & ready for firing. 2/Lt BRIGLEY, C.G. reported sick 8/9/16 & was returned to duty 15/9/16.	

WAR DIARY
or
INTELLIGENCE SUMMARY.
(Erase heading not required.)

Instructions regarding War Diaries and Intelligence Summaries are contained in F. S. Regs., Part II. and the Staff Manual respectively. Title pages will be prepared in manuscript.

Place	Date	Hour	Summary of Events and Information	Remarks and references to Appendices
	25 August 16			
			1652 Pte Farr T. admitted to Hospital 10/8/16	
			2219 Cpl Lee J. —"— 11/8/16	
			4065 Pte Crossan H. —"— 16/8/16	
			1657 Pte Furno S. —"— 17/8/16	
			1844 Pte Hall W. —"— 20/8/16	
			3336 Pte O'Hara G. —"— 21/8/16	
			2790 Pte Mallinson W. —"— 23/8/16	
			3308 Pte Martin J. —"— 25/8/16	
			3214 Pte Kershaw F. —"— 28/8/16	
			SICK	

WAR DIARY
or
INTELLIGENCE SUMMARY.

(Erase heading not required.)

Place	Date	Hour	Summary of Events and Information	Remarks and references to Appendices
THIEPVAL LEFT SECTOR ARQUÈVES	Aug 26	1 pm	The Battery was relieved by 74 T.M.B. & they marched to ARQUÈVES	
	27		Training in use of Stokes mortar in the attack	
do., FORCEVILLE	27		At 4.30 pm the Battery marched to FORCEVILLE	
FORCEVILLE	28		Church Parade in morning. Gun Drill	
	29		One Section relieved 146 T.M.B. in the line between THIEPVAL AVENUE (excl.) & SANDY AVENUE (incl.) — the remainder stays at FORCEVILLE.	
THIEPVAL (Right)	30		Section relieved and went into Reserve at NORTH BLUFF	#1
			Remainder section at Forceville	#2
—	31		Section at Forceville moved to NORTH BLUFF	#3
			4104 Pte Mahar 16 admitted to hospital	#4

AWilmurd Lt.
for O.C. 147 T.M.B.

www.ingramcontent.com/pod-product-compliance
Lightning Source LLC
Chambersburg PA
CBHW081510160426
43193CB00014B/2639